The Alligator's Red Shoes

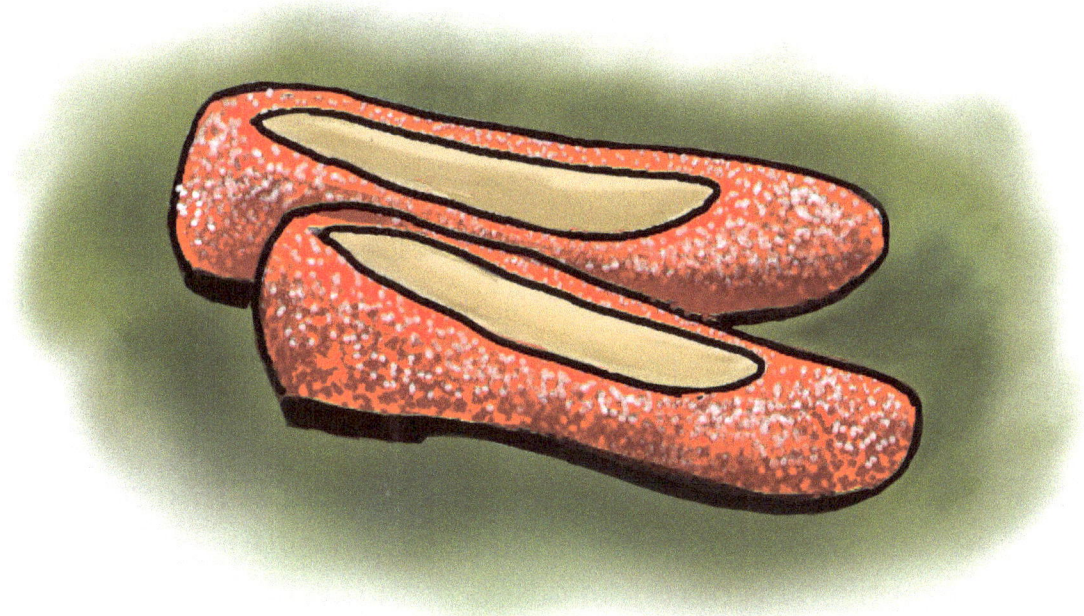

Jim Munroe

Illustrated by Samantha Bell

The Alligator's Red Shoes
ISBN: Softcover 978-1-960326-55-3
Copyright © 2024 by Jim Munroe

All rights reserved. No part of this book may be reproduced or transmitted in any form or by any means, electronic or mechanical, including photocopying, recording, or by any information storage and retrieval system, without permission in writing from the publisher.

Parson's Porch Books is an imprint of Parson's Porch & Company (PP&C) in Cleveland, Tennessee. PP&C is a self-funded charity which earns money by publishing books of noted authors, representing all genres. Its face and voice is **David Russell Tullock** who you can contact at: dtullock@parsonsporch.com

Parson's Porch & Company *turns books into bread & milk* by sharing its profits with the poor.

www.parsonsporch.com

The Alligator's Red Shoes

It had a sly grin that went ear to ear
With a wink of his eye, I had nothing to fear.
So I told the gator," Please pull up a seat
And tell me about those shoes on your feet."

The gator said, "My dear friend,
   with long furry hair
Have a seat on the floor
   and my story I'll share.
Quite some time ago
   as I seem to recall,
The leaves had turned color,
   it must have been fall.

The river rolled by as I napped by the shore
Then I heard a small splash and went to explore.
A dad with two daughters paddled by in a boat
So I slipped in the water and started to float.

Dad pulled both the oars
   with a nice easy stroke
The girls sat in back
   telling joke after joke.

One daughter had blonde hair, the other had black
Each one of them carried a pack on their back.
But as I drew closer and looked down my nose,
I saw sparkling red shoes that covered their toes.

I must have those shoes,
　　so I better think quick
And dove under water
　　and started to kick.
I swam faster and gave
　　the boat a big bump
That made those girls scream
　　and they started to jump.

Then I splashed the boat until they were all wet
And I must admit they were pretty upset!

Dad paddled hard but I stayed right by their side
And I opened my mouth so big and so wide.
Dad yelled at the girls "Hurry! Open your packs
And throw him our lunch and all of our snacks!"

I caught each one just as the other young girl
Had taken her shoes and gave them a big whirl.

Her red shoes flew high and tumbled and sailed
And they all landed on the end of my tail.

Dad started rowing
   and down the river they flew
And I drifted to shore
   with two pairs of shoes.

I tried each one on and they fit me just right
Not one was too loose and not one was too tight.

So I started walking from town after town
Shopping and searching and just looking around.
I have looked high and low in so many stores
My scaly feet are just a little bit sore."

Well I sat there amazed at this story I heard
How could I believe even one single word?
So I asked the gator as it walked out the door,

www.ingramcontent.com/pod-product-compliance
Lightning Source LLC
Chambersburg PA
CBHW061350010526
44107CB00011B/887